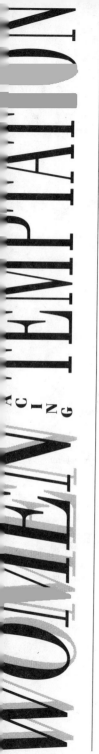

WOMEN AND TEMPTATION

Cindy Bunch

12 studies for
individuals or groups

CREATED MALE & FEMALE BIBLE STUDIES

*With Study Notes & Guidelines
for Leaders*

INTERVARSITY PRESS
DOWNERS GROVE, ILLINOIS 60515

To my mother, who has shown me what it means
to be a woman of God.

InterVarsity Press® is the book-publishing division of InterVarsity Christian Fellowship®, a student movement active on campus at hundreds of universities, colleges and schools of nursing in the United States of America, and a member movement of the International Fellowship of Evangelical Students. For information about local and regional activities, write Public Relations Dept., Inter-Varsity Christian Fellowship, 6400 Schroeder Rd., P.O. Box 7895, Madison, WI 53707-7895.

Cover photograph: Michael Goss

ISBN 0-8308-1138-9

Printed in the United States of America ∞

15	14	13	12	11	10	9	8	7	6	5	4	3	2
03	02	01	00	99	98	97	96	95	94	93			

Getting the Most out of Created Male & Female Bible Studies

Created Male and Female Bible Studies are designed to help us understand what it means to be created in the image of God. We know that God had a purpose in creating two sexes. Discovering gender distinctions is an exciting and intriguing part of what it means to be human. But sometimes it is confusing and frustrating as well. These studies will help us understand what God's purpose is for us individually and as a part of the human race.

The passages you will study will be challenging, inspiring and practical. They will show you how to think about your sexuality and how you live that out. And they will help you to better understand what the other sex is about—breaking down stereotypes and helping you find new ways to communicate.

These guides are not designed merely to convince you of the truthfulness of some idea held by the authors. Rather, they are intended to guide you into discovering biblical truths that will renew your heart and mind. How? Through an inductive approach to Bible study. Rather than simply telling you what they believe, the authors will lead you to discover what the Bible says about a particular topic through a series of questions. These studies will help you to think about the meaning of the passage so that you can truly understand what the biblical writer intended to say.

Additionally, these studies are personal. At the end of each study, you'll be given an opportunity to make a commitment to respond—to take steps toward changing the way you think and act. And you'll find guidance for prayer as well.

Finally, these studies are versatile. They are designed for student, professional, neighborhood and/or church groups. They are also effective for individual study.

How They're Put Together

Created Male and Female Bible Studies have a distinctive workbook format with space for writing a response to each question. This format is ideal for personal study and allows group members to prepare in advance for the discussion or write down notes during the study. Each study takes about forty-five minutes in a group setting or thirty minutes in personal study—unless you choose to take more time.

At the end of the guide are some study notes. They do not give "the answers," but they do provide additional background information on certain questions to help you through the difficult spots. In addition, the "Guidelines for Leaders" section describes how to lead a group discussion, gives helpful tips on group dynamics and suggests ways to deal with problems which may arise during the discussion. With such helps, someone with little or no experience can lead an effective group study.

Suggestions for Individual Study

1. As you begin the study, pray that God will help you understand the passage and apply it to your life. Ask him to show you what kinds of action to take as a result of your time of study.

2. In your first session take time to read the introduction to the entire guide. This will orient you to the subject at hand and to the author's goals for the studies.

3. Read the short introduction to the study.

4. Read and reread the suggested Bible passage to familiarize yourself with it.

5. A good modern translation of the Bible will give you the most help. The New International Version, the New American Standard Bible and the New Revised Standard Version are all recommended. The questions in this guide are based on the New International Version.

6. Use the space provided to jot your answers to the questions. This will help you express your understanding of the passage clearly.

7. Take time with the final questions and the "Respond" section in each study to commit yourself to action and/or a change in attitude. You may wish to find a study partner to discuss your insights with, one who will keep you accountable for the commitments you make.

Suggestions for Members of a Group Study

1. Come to the study prepared. Follow the suggestions for individual study mentioned above. You will find that careful preparation will greatly enrich your time spent in group discussion.

2. Be willing to participate in the discussion. The leader of your group will not be lecturing. Instead, he or she will be encouraging the members of the group to discuss what they have learned. The leader will be asking the questions that are found in this guide.

3. Stick to the topic being discussed. Your answers should be based on the verses which are the focus of the discussion.

4. Be sensitive to the other members of the group. Listen attentively when they describe what they have learned. You may be surprised by their insights! When possible, link what you say to the comments of others. Also, be affirming whenever you can. This will encourage some of the more hesitant members of the group to participate.

5. Be careful not to dominate the discussion. We are sometimes so eager to express our thoughts that we leave too little opportunity for others to respond. By all means participate! But allow others to do so as well.

6. Expect God to teach you through the passage being discussed and through the other members of the group. Pray that you will have an enjoyable and profitable time together, but also that as a result of the study you will find ways you can take action individually and/or as a group.

7. Be ready to make a personal application of the principles in the study. The final questions will guide you in this. Although you may or may not wish to discuss the "Respond" section as a group, you may want to hold one another accountable in some way for those personal commitments.
8. We recommend that groups agree to follow a few basic guidelines, and that these be read at the beginning of the first session. You may wish to adapt the following guidelines to your situation:

☐ Anything personal which is shared in the group is considered confidential and will not be discussed outside the group unless specific permission is given to do so.

☐ We will provide time for each person present to talk if he or she feels comfortable doing so.

☐ We will talk about ourselves and our own situations, avoiding conversation about other people.

☐ We will listen attentively to each other.

☐ We will be very cautious about giving advice.

☐ We will pray for each other.

If you are the group leader, you will find additional suggestions at the back of the guide.

How the Series Works

Where should you start? If you'd like to go through several guides in the series, whether with a group or individually, a good place to start is *Sexual Wholeness.* This guide will give you a good overview of the issues, and you may find various areas you want to explore further. While *Sexual Wholeness* may be used in either same-sex or mixed (male and female) groups, it may be uncomfortable for some in mixed groups. As a companion to that guide, you may wish to use *Created for Relationships.* If you are in a mixed group, this may be a more comfortable starting place.

Created Female and *Created Male* are designed for same-sex groups but could be used together for enlightening discussions in mixed groups. To facilitate this use, studies three through five are the same in both guides. The other studies could be intermixed so that group members have a unique opportunity to hear the perspective, needs and struggles of the other sex.

Women Facing Temptation and *Men Facing Temptation* are also designed for same-sex groups but could be adapted for use in mixed groups. You will find that all the temptations covered are applicable to either gender. This could be an opportunity for interesting discussion about how these temptations are both similar and distinct for each sex. You may discover new ways to support each other and help one another avoid temptation.

For two quarters of study on how we live out our gender roles, *Roles in Ministry* and *Following God Together* make good study companions. *Roles in Ministry* looks specifically at the role of women in the church by studying the relevant passages and is designed to help the reader find a unique place of service. Through a series of character studies involving pairs of men and women, *Following God Together* will help us see the temptations and frustrations men and women find in service together and the great possibilities for ministry when abilities are combined.

Introducing *Women Facing Temptation*

We live in a superficial culture. Being a woman in our culture brings a unique set of pressures and demands. The only way we can keep up is to try to be superhuman. We may think we should have it all—a strong career, an ideal family, a great personality and a perfect figure. As a result, we feel that we are inadequate. We begin to think we'll never measure up to the ideal.

But we have taken our standard from the world and left God's standard behind.

According to our culture, we should not be content with what we have, but always strive for more—more money, popularity and power. Yet working toward these goals doesn't lead to satisfaction. Instead, we may begin to worry or become bitter about our situation. And this leads to destructive behavior like jealousy and gossip.

Another problem created by following the world's values is that we are not allowed to be ourselves. Instead, our culture outlines certain kinds of behavior which are "appropriate" for women. For example, the world tells us that we should be passive. But God wants us to be assertively working to bring his kingdom into reality.

The world tells us that we should use manipulation to get what we want. But God wants honesty and openness from us.

The world tells us that we should put the highest value on pleasing the people we care about—no matter what the cost is to us. But God wants us to put him first.

Women have a multitude of difficult temptations to face in the world each day. And once we allow ourselves to fall into one of these patterns, several of the others will pull us in as well. These Bible studies pinpoint some of these vulnerable areas so that we can face them head on.

Trying to fit into the world's expectations causes us to lose some of our creativity and limits our ability to serve God. However, through Christ and the support we have in his body, the church, we can begin to do battle with these temptations. Once we do, we will be freed to serve him more fully.

Cindy Bunch

1
Low Self-Esteem

Psalm 139:13-16

*I*f we try to meet the standards of our superficial world, we will always eventually fail. Unfortunately, this may cause us to think that we are not adequate. We forget that we are fearfully and wonderfully made by a loving Creator.

In *Good Morning, Merry Sunshine,* Bob Greene describes his amazing newborn daughter:

> The fingernails are the thing. Everything about the baby is amazing, but when I look at her fingernails—so small you couldn't even measure them on a ruler, but perfectly formed—that's when the miracle hits home again every time. And it's not just me. When people come into the apartment and see Amanda for the first time, they invariably end up saying, "Look at those fingernails."
>
> I'd take a picture of them, but they wouldn't show up.[1]

All of us, like Amanda, have particular gifts which set us apart. This is how our Lord has made us.

Open

Each of us has unique physical, emotional, mental and spiritual qualities. And it is important for us to recognize our gifts from our Creator in each of these areas.

☐ Name one gift you have in each of these areas. The following lists will help you get started:

Physical	Emotional	Mental	Spiritual
feet	listening	remembering	praying
hands	stability	analyzing	encouraging
figure	patience	comparing	healing
face	empathizing	contrasting	teaching
mouth	supporting	calculating	meditating
hair	encouraging	interpreting	giving

☐ How did you feel about doing this exercise? (embarrassed? pleased? encouraged? Was it easy or difficult for you?)

Study

Read Psalm 139:13-16.

1. What picture of the Creator God does this passage give you?

2. Looking through the whole passage, in what periods of life do you see God playing a role?

3. What is meant by the phrase "inmost being" in verse 13?

4. In verse 14 the author says, "Your works are wonderful, I know that full well." Name some other works of God which are wonderful.

How do you feel when compared to these other works of God? (You are "fearfully and wonderfully made.")

5. The "secret place" in verse 15 is a reference to the womb. How do you feel when you know that God saw you even there?

6. How do you understand the idea that our days are ordained (v. 16)?

How does this affect how you understand God's purposes for you?

7. In what ways do you need to reform your self-understanding to make it more consistent with who God created you to be?

Respond
Take time in prayer to thank God for the good things you have seen in yourself as a result of this study. Pray also that he will continue to make his attitudes your attitudes.

---

[1]Bob Greene, *Good Morning, Merry Sunshine* (New York: Macmillan, 1984), p. 26.

2
Discontent

Psalm 77:1-15

*T*he room is too cold. Why were we seated way back in the corner? You'd think a restaurant like this would have more selection on the menu. When is our food going to get here? I don't even think this waitress deserves a tip . . ."

Perhaps you've had a meal with a person who complains like this. Some people are never satisfied with what they are given. Such people are tiring to be with. In contrast, the person who is aware of God's never-ending good gifts (often a person who seems to have comparatively less) is a joy to be around.

Where do you fall on this spectrum?

Open
☐ Name three things you're grateful for.

☐ Reflect on your response. (How long did it take you to think of things you're grateful for? Did they come to mind quickly or slowly? How conscious are you of God's good gifts?) What did you learn about yourself?

Study
Read Psalm 77:1-15.
1. How would you describe the tone of verses 1-9?

2. What words and phrases does the psalmist use to describe his emotion?

3. Why does he "groan" at the memory of God (vv. 3-9)?

4. The psalmist's discontent makes him "too troubled to speak." When have you experienced this?

5. How does the tone change in verses 10-15?

6. What is the source of the change?

7. How is God described in verses 10-15?

8. Sometimes our culture leads us to believe that material things and achievements, such as a promotion at work, social status, the right relationship, a new car or the perfect house, will bring contentment. What false sources of contentment do you put faith in?

What in this passage could help you reform your thinking?

Respond
The psalmist finds his source of contentment in who God is. Make God's character—rather than your needs—a focus of prayer this week.

3
Gossip

James 3:3-12

*O*ne of the wonders of a circus is the ability of the lion tamer to control such a huge and powerful beast with the aid of only a whip and a chair. Part of the excitement of the circus is knowing that if anything went wrong, the result could be deadly for the lion tamer and perhaps for others.

In a similar way our tongues must be tamed. Although they are small, like the lion our tongues have great power—which can be used for good or for evil. When our tongues are not under control, many people around us are hurt by our words.

"Thelma? You'll never guess who needs our prayers and why!"

Open
Although the point is made gently, most of us can probably see ourselves in the cartoon on page 19.
☐ How do you rationalize gossip?

☐ When is sharing information about others acceptable?

☐ What damage have you seen from gossip?

☐ How do you feel when you hear other people gossiping?

Study
Read James 3:3-12.
1. List the comparisons made in verses 3-6.

2. What is the purpose of these comparisons (v. 5)?

3. The image of fire is used repeatedly in these verses. In what ways is the work of the tongue a fire spreading through (and corrupting) the whole person?

4. We can tame wild animals. Why is it that the tongue is such a "restless evil" that no one can tame it?

5. How does the author contrast the positive and negative uses of the tongue (vv. 9-12)?

6. In verse 12 we read, "Neither can a salt spring produce fresh water." How do gossip and malicious talk affect your ability to worship God?

7. When are you tempted to gossip?

8. How can we keep our tongues from controlling us?

Respond
Ask someone you trust and respect to help you monitor your tongue as you try to use it to encourage and uplift the people around you.

4
Bitterness

Ephesians 4:25-32

Do not hate your brother in your heart. . . . Do not seek revenge or bear a grudge against one of your people, but love your neighbor as yourself" (Leviticus 19:17-18).

We know that we should be forgiving and not be bitter. But sometimes situations overwhelm us, and we don't know what to do with our anger. At other times we begin to enjoy wallowing in our anger, and we allow it to develop into bitterness. Anger can be doubly difficult for women because it is a "forbidden" emotion. We may have learned to suppress anger so well that we don't even realize we're experiencing it. For this reason, bitterness is a common temptation for women.

Dale and Juanita Ryan describe bitterness as "an intense animosity toward another person that erodes our peace of mind and robs us of joy."[1] We need to be rid of bitterness because of how it affects us—and because of how it affects all of our relationships.

Open
☐ When are you most likely to get angry?

☐ When do you experience bitterness?

☐ What do you think is the difference between anger and bitterness?

Study
Read Ephesians 4:25-32.
1. List the negative behaviors mentioned in these verses.

List the positive behaviors.

2. Verse 25 tells us we are to speak truthfully because we are all members of the same body. Why is it important for Christians to be honest with each other?

3. What do you learn from verses 26-27 about handling anger?

4. How do you think we can get angry without sinning?

5. What kinds of things would qualify as unwholesome talk?

6. In verse 26 we are told to be careful how we handle anger. In verse 31 we are told to get rid of anger. How do we know whether our anger needs to be expressed or let go of?

7. When is it difficult for you to express your anger?

8. When is it hard for you to forgive someone you are angry with?

What do you find in these verses to help you with forgiveness?

Respond
Given what you have learned about yourself through this study, work toward developing new strategies for handling your anger and avoiding bitterness.

---

[1]Dale and Juanita Ryan, *Recovery from Bitterness* (Downers Grove, Ill.: InterVarsity Press, 1990), p. 11.

5
Lust

Ephesians 5:1-10

A friend of mine was talking about a new music video by one of his favorite female artists. He described one scene that he found particularly seductive. The gorgeous singer was standing under a waterfall. His very honest response was to say, "I *really* wanted to be the water."

Sometimes it's easier to discern a man's lustful behavior because men are stimulated by the visual. Women, on the other hand, are said to be stimulated by touch, personality and words. What has your experience been? Whether we fit into these gender categories or not, we need to know what makes us vulnerable.

Open
What do you think lust is? Create a definition or choose from the responses on the next page and explain your answer.

☐ Daydreaming about being sexually intimate with your spouse.

☐ Thinking about what it would be like to have sex with someone you are dating seriously.

☐ Thinking about what it would be like to be sexually intimate with someone other than your spouse.

☐ Noticing someone you find sexually appealing and desiring to get to know that person.

☐ Approaching someone in a public setting and introducing yourself simply because you find the person sexually attractive.

☐ Finding yourself drawn to a person you know—or to a celebrity of some sort—and trying to arrange things so that you can see or be with that person.

☐ Staring at another person's body.

☐ Watching a sexually explicit or pornographic movie.

Study

Read Ephesians 5:1-10.

1. List all of the commands in these verses.

2. The word *love* is repeated three times in the first two verses. Why do you think it is used so frequently?

3. Passion is an appropriate part of love, when a man and a woman delight in each other physically in marriage. How would you contrast the passion of love with the passion of lust as it is described in verses 3-9?

4. Verse 3 says that among Christians "there must not be even a hint of sexual immorality." What qualifies as a hint of sexual immorality in your view?

5. This is a difficult standard to meet. In what ways do you find it difficult to uphold?

6. According to verse 4, what kinds of actions qualify as inappropriate behaviors?

7. Verse 4 tells us that we should replace these behaviors with thanksgiving. Why do you think this is? (See v. 5.)

8. How can the kinds of people described in verses 5-6 lead us into sexual immorality, coarse joking and impure thoughts?

9. Verses 8-10 tell us, in contrast, how we should live as children of light. What do you need to do to bring your lustful thoughts and actions out of the darkness and into the light?

Respond
Consider how the media prompt us to lustful thoughts through advertising, TV shows, movies and so on. What step can you take to begin to monitor what you take into your mind?

6
Passivity

2 Timothy 1:6-12

Women are often taught to not be confrontational. Maintaining close relationships is often our highest value. In order not to create friction in our significant relationships, we often conform to what others want us to do, putting our own desires aside.

Sounds noble, doesn't it?

In reality, these behaviors may simply be masking our fears and our reluctance to make tough decisions. We are not serving Christ in the way he has called us to serve.

Open
☐ When is it hard for you to take initiative and use your skills and talents in your family relationships?

with friends?

at work?

at church?

Study
Read 2 Timothy 1:6-12.
1. What key words do you notice repeated in these verses?

2. According to this passage, what are some characteristics of the power of the gospel?

3. What does verse 6 tell us about the gifts we are given?

4. Verse 7 tells us that we are not given a spirit of timidity, but of power, love and self-discipline (also translated as *self-control* and *a sound mind*). How do these three gifts help us face timidity?

5. Paul was in prison and the other believers had deserted him. They feared Nero's wrath on them as well. When have you found it difficult to testify of God?

6. In the context of your temperament, do you experience and demonstrate passivity? If so, how?

7. How can verses 8-10 and 12 encourage you when you feel timid about using your gifts?

8. Like Paul, we are heralds of the gospel. How are you being a witness to the truth by fanning into flame the gift that God has given you?

9. How could your life better reflect the power that is within you?

Respond

Monitor your responses to various people and situations. When is it hard for you to express your desires? When is it hard for you to use your skills? Begin to pray for the courage to change these patterns so that you can serve God with boldness.

7

Worry

Joshua 1:1-9

Someone once did some research and concluded that of the things we worry about:

—40% will never happen.

—30% concern old decisions which cannot be altered.

—12% center on criticisms, mostly untrue, made by people who feel inferior.

—10% are related to personal health—which worsens when we worry.

—8% are "legitimate" and can be met head-on when we have eliminated senseless worries.

Whether our worries are "legitimate" or not, Christ is interested in comforting us when we worry. Better yet, he is waiting for us to submit our concerns to his power. We do not have to solve life's problems alone.

Open

☐ What have you worried about recently?

☐ Under which of the above categories does it fit?

☐ Is this an area you often worry about? If not, what kinds of things cause you the most worry?

Why do you think you worry about these things?

Study
Read Joshua 1:1-9.
1. From what you read in these verses, what do you gather about what has happened up to this point? (Who is being addressed? What important events have taken place and will take place in the future?)

2. What do you think Joshua would have been feeling at this time?

3. List all the promises God makes in these verses.

4. How would these promises have encouraged Joshua?

5. What is commanded (vv. 6-9)?

6. The "Book of the Law" is a reference to the laws which were given at Mount Sinai. We have available to us the entire Old and New Testaments, which tell us what God wants from us. How can meditating on God's law keep you from worrying?

7. Verse 9 says "do not be terrified," which suggests that their worries were at an extreme point. Often our worries grow way out of proportion. Think back to the area of worry you named in the open question. In what ways do you need to take courage and trust in God to be with you?

Respond

Begin to notice the "early warning signals" of worry. Realistically categorize your worry and then begin to deal with it before God, before it begins to affect your ability to serve him. As you pray, remember these words from Philippians 4:6-7:

> Do not be anxious about anything, but in everything, by prayer and petition, with thanksgiving, present your requests to God. And the peace of God, which transcends all understanding, will guard your hearts and your minds in Christ Jesus.

8
Materialism

Ecclesiastes 5:10-20

A mansion. A helicopter. A Rolls Royce. Servants all over the place. A huge swimming pool. And the caption on the poster I saw in the store reads, "He who dies with the most toys wins."

A friend of mine proudly wears a shirt bearing the words "Shop 'til you drop."

At first glance, I found both of these sayings very funny. However, they are also a very serious commentary on the values of our culture. Christians may not openly claim these values, but we too may lust after material wealth.

Open
☐ How would you define materialism?

☐ How do you think the Bible calls us to regard our money and possessions?

☐ Give an example of how your beliefs about material wealth affected a decision you recently made.

Study
Read Ecclesiastes 5:10-20.
1. What uses of wealth are described in negative terms in these verses?

2. What is the basic principle described in verses 10-12?

3. How have you seen this principle to be true in your life?

4. Why do you think the author says "the sleep of a laborer is sweet"?

5. What do verses 15-16 tell us about wealth?

6. The tone changes in verses 18-20. What is different about these verses?

7. How have you seen wealth used for the good of the kingdom?

8. In what ways are you tempted to love money and/or material things?

9. How do you need to change your lifestyle?

Respond
Keep track of everything you buy or spend money on for one month. (Try to follow your normal patterns of spending.) At the end of the month sit down and evaluate your expenses. We can always improve in this area. How could you become a better steward of the money God has given you?

9
People-Pleasing

Galatians 1:6-10

Kevin Leman's book *The Pleasers* opens with the following story about a woman in counseling:

She's "successful" as wife, mother, and working woman. She is busy, oh, so busy. Her schedule rivals the man who rides around in Air Force One. It seems her kids are involved in every activity and sport, and therefore so is she.

Her husband? Well, he's busy too, even busier than she is. He works long hours, staggers in anywhere from 7:30 to 9:45 P.M., sometimes too tired to eat, always ready to collapse on the couch and watch TV. She doesn't say anything, of course, because when she does he can get quite angry.

This woman seems to have it all, so "Why," she asks, "am I so depressed? Why don't my kids listen to me? Why can't I say no?"[1]

Most women can probably identify in some way with this woman's dilemma. Are you a people-pleaser?

Open
□ *The Pleasers* has a self-test to help readers determine how oriented to pleasing they are. Which of the following characteristics describe you?

_I feel insecure and not very confident much of the time.

_I have to "walk on eggs" to keep everyone from getting angry.

_I feel overpowered by the people I'm close to.

_I'm always saying "I should have" or "I ought to."

_I don't like confrontations. They're just too unpleasant.

_I often fake it and tell others I like what they're doing or saying when I really don't.

_If I try on six or seven pairs of shoes at the store, I feel obligated to buy at least one pair.

_I feel as if I'm not really running my own life.

_I am easily talked into choices that please other people more than they please me.[2]

□ Why do you think you fall into these patterns?

Study
Read Galatians 1:6-10.

1. What words show the passionate nature of Paul's arguments in these verses?

2. From these verses, how would you describe the people Paul is addressing?

3. What is pulling them away from Christ (vv. 6-7)?

4. In what ways do people pull you away from the grace that is offered to you in Christ?

5. How do we try to win the approval of other people?

6. Why does Paul say he wouldn't be a servant of Christ if he were still trying to win the approval of people (v. 10)?

7. In verse 6 we are reminded that we are called by the grace of Christ. We serve a loving God. How does this motivate you to please him?

8. In what ways does pleasing God require that you stop trying to please those around you? (Consider Christian family members and friends as well as non-Christians.)

Respond
Begin to change your patterns of people-pleasing by making one choice this week that you know pleases God (even when others want something different) and one choice that pleases you (like telling your friends which movie you *really* want to see with them, when they ask for your preference).

---

[1]Kevin Leman, *The Pleasers* (New York: Dell Publishing, 1987), pp. 3-4.
[2]Adapted from Leman, *The Pleasers*, pp. 20-21.

10
Manipulation

1 Kings 21:1-19

A recent book by a Christian publisher entitled *Not Just Any Man: A Guide to Finding Mr. Right* explains that the way to find a husband is to practice careful manipulation. For example, the author suggests that a woman should compliment men often. At the office she could say, "I really think you are the best salesman in the company." At church she might "comment on how much more perceptive he is than others or how much more he's thought through his beliefs than other men." The author concludes by saying, "Of course you should base your comparison on some supporting evidence, but don't be too literal."

This kind of advice to women is not new. But since Old Testament days the results of manipulation have been both sin and compromise.

Open
☐ What kinds of actions define manipulation?

☐ Think of a time when you manipulated events to your advantage. What factors prompted you to do this?

☐ How are we able to rationalize manipulative actions?

Study
Read 1 Kings 21:1-19.
1. How does Ahab present his request in verses 1-2?

2. Naboth refuses because he believes the land has been given to his family by the Lord, and he wants to keep it as his family's inheritance in the Promised Land. Describe Ahab's response from verse 4.

3. How does Jezebel react to her husband's behavior (vv. 5-7)?

4. In what ways do you think Ahab's behavior was manipulative?

5. How does Jezebel attempt to resolve the problem (vv. 8-16)?

6. After Ahab's direct approach fails, Jezebel is able to manipulate the situation to Ahab's advantage. Sometimes manipulation seems to work. However, what is the end result (vv. 17-19)?

7. How might the pressures of our culture encourage women to use manipulative tactics to achieve their goals and desires?

8. When are you tempted to manipulate situations to your own advantage or that of people close to you?

What would be a more Christlike approach to those kinds of situations?

Respond
Recognizing the manipulative patterns in your life is a major step in overcoming them. Seek help from supportive friends who can hold you accountable as you begin to work toward correcting these patterns. And ask God to give you insight and courage.

11
Jealousy

Genesis 15:2-6; 16:1-6

*I*n *Temptations Women Face* the author tells the following story:
I was in California visiting Kris who longs to be married. Saturday evening she and I talked in her apartment. She told me, tears running down her cheeks, "You know, I really find it hard not to envy you your husband, and your family, your home. I'm nearly forty and I feel incomplete. . . . This feeling inside, of wanting something so badly and seeing other people who take it for granted . . . sometimes it eats me up."[1]

Women often experience jealousy like this, and the effects are devastating—relationally, emotionally, even physically. How can we be freed of this leechlike sin?

Open
☐ The following are some ways envy shows up in our lives. Which of these affect you? Explain your choices.

_Comparing yourself to someone more successful and feeling unhappy about his or her success.

_Feeling that you deserve what you envy.

_Finding yourself wanting to put down successful people by gossiping about them.

_Avoiding seeing other people's successes.

_Wanting to gain from other people's losses.[2]

_Desiring to have what another person has and dwelling on that desire.

_Focusing on imitating someone you see as more successful because you want to have what that person has achieved.

☐ What is the difference between envying someone and having a role model?

☐ When are you most vulnerable to envy?

☐ Why do you think women are vulnerable to envy?

Study
Read Genesis 15:2-6 and 16:1-6.
1. What promise does God make to Abraham in 15:4-5?

2. In 16:1 we learn that Abram and Sarai still have no children. What does Sarai decide to do?

3. What do the actions they take in verses 2-4 reveal about Sarai and Abram?

4. Why do you think Hagar responded to Sarai as she did (v. 4)?

5. Describe Abram's response to Sarai's complaint (vv. 5-6).

6. Verse 6 says that Sarai "mistreated" Hagar, implying that Sarai was unjust. Why do you think she did this?

7. Although Hagar apparently held some blame since she despised her mistress, it does seem that Sarai responded with jealousy to the situation she had initiated (Hagar's pregnancy). When do you most often experience jealousy?

8. How can we keep our jealousy from causing us to mistreat people?

9. With what positive emotions and goals would you like to replace your envy?

Respond
Pick one person toward whom you often feel jealous. Try to find out what his or her needs are. (Remember, everyone has areas of hurt and concern.) Begin to pray regularly for that person. Reevaluate your attitude in two weeks.

---

[1]Mary Ellen Ashcroft, *Temptations Women Face* (Downers Grove, Ill.: InterVarsity Press, 1991), p. 143.
[2]Adapted from Betsy Cohen, *The Snow White Syndrome: All About Envy* (New York: Macmillan, 1986), p. 21.

12
Complacency

Hebrews 5:11—6:3

Spiritual growth requires effort. It means rejecting the trivial activities that keep us running frantically like someone who can't get off a treadmill. Instead, when the speed on the treadmill gets higher and higher, we try to keep up. What we need to do is to jump off the treadmill.

Mary Ellen Ashcroft points out that originally the word *sloth,* which we equate with laziness, meant "spiritual lethargy." She says, "When I don't bother to spend time with God or don't care about my relationship with God, when I allow other activities to take priority over my relationship with God, then I am tempted by sloth."[1] This is the essence of complacency.

Open
☐ What keeps you on your "treadmill"?

☐ How could you better use the time and talent God has given you?

Study
Read Hebrews 5:11—6:3.

1. Describe the people who are being addressed in these verses.

2. The recipients of this letter are described as "slow to learn" (5:11). What might cause this?

3. What are the basic reasons for their immaturity (5:11-14)?

4. What teachings do they need to move beyond in order to reach maturity (6:1-2)?

Why would it be important for them to move beyond these teachings?

5. The author tells the readers that if they continue to yearn only for milk they will never grow. What is spiritual milk?

6. Why might some people want to have only milk?

7. What kinds of things qualify as spiritual solid food?

8. In what ways do you need to move on in your Christian life?

Respond

Find someone to hold you accountable in the area you mentioned above. Ask that person to check in with you regularly.

---

[1]Ashcroft, *Temptations Women Face*, p. 87.

Guidelines for Leaders

Leading a Bible discussion can be an enjoyable and rewarding experience. But it can also be intimidating—especially if you've never done it before. If this is how you feel, you're in good company.

Remember when God asked Moses to lead the Israelites out of Egypt? Moses replied, "O Lord, please send someone else to do it" (Exodus 4:13). But God gave Moses the help (human and divine) he needed to be a strong leader.

Leading a Bible discussion is not difficult if you follow certain guidelines. You don't need to be an expert on the Bible or a trained teacher. The suggestions listed below can help you to effectively fulfill your role as leader—and enjoy doing it.

Preparing for the Study
1. As you study the passage ahead of time, ask God to help you understand it and apply it in your own life. Unless this happens, you will not be prepared to lead others. Pray too for the various members of the group. Ask God to open your hearts to the message of his Word and motivate you to action.
2. Read the introduction to the entire guide to get an overview of the subject at hand and the issues which will be explored.
3. Be ready for the "Open" questions with a personal story or example. The group will be only as vulnerable and open as its leader.

4. As you begin preparing for each study, read and reread the assigned Bible passage to familiarize yourself with it.

5. This study guide is based on the New International Version of the Bible. It will help you and the group if you use this translation as the basis for your study and discussion.

6. Carefully work through each question in the study. Spend time in meditation and reflection as you consider how to respond.

7. Write your thoughts and responses in the space provided in the study guide. This will help you to express your understanding of the passage clearly.

8. It might help you to have a Bible dictionary handy. Use it to look up any unfamiliar words, names or places. (For additional help on how to study a passage, see chapter five of *Leading Bible Discussions, IVP.*)

9. Take the final (application) questions and the "Respond" portion of each study seriously. Consider what this means for your life—what changes you may need to make in your lifestyle and/or actions you can take in your church or with people you know. Remember that the group will follow your lead in responding to the studies.

Leading the Study

1. Be sure everyone in your group has a study guide and Bible. Encourage the group to prepare beforehand for each discussion by reading the introduction to the guide and by working through the questions in the study.

2. At the beginning of your first time together, explain that these studies are meant to be discussions, not lectures. Encourage the members of the group to participate. However, do not put pressure on those who may be hesitant to speak during the first few sessions.

3. Begin the study on time. Open with prayer, asking God to help the group understand and apply the passage.

4. Have a group member read the introductory paragraph at the beginning of the discussion. This will remind the group of the topic of the study.

5. Every study begins with a section called "Open." These "approach" questions are meant to be asked before the passage is read. They are important for several reasons.

First, there is always a stiffness that needs to be overcome before people will begin to talk openly. A good question will break the ice.

Second, most people will have lots of different things going on in their minds (dinner, an exam, an important meeting coming up, how to get the car fixed) that have nothing to do with the study. A creative question will get their attention and draw them into the discussion.

Third, approach questions can reveal where our thoughts or feelings need to be transformed by Scripture. That is why it is especially important not to read the passage before the approach question is asked. The passage will tend to color the honest reactions people would otherwise give, because they feel they are supposed to think the way the Bible does.

6. Have a group member read aloud the passage to be studied.

7. As you ask the questions, keep in mind that they are designed to be used just as they are written. You may simply read them aloud. Or you may prefer to express them in your own words.

There may be times when it is appropriate to deviate from the study guide. For example, a question may already have been answered. If so, move on to the next question. Or someone may raise an important question not covered in the guide. Take time to discuss it, but try to keep the group from going off on tangents.

8. Avoid answering your own questions. Repeat or rephrase them if necessary until they are clearly understood. An eager group quickly becomes passive and silent if members think the leader will give all the "right" answers.

9. Don't be afraid of silence. People may need time to think about the question before formulating their answers.

10. Don't be content with just one answer. Ask "What do the rest of you think?" or "Anything else?" until several people have given answers to a question.

11. Acknowledge all contributions. Be affirming whenever possible. Never reject an answer. If it is clearly off base, ask "Which verse led you to that conclusion?" or "What do the rest of you think?"

12. Don't expect every answer to be addressed to you, even though this will probably happen at first. As group members become more at ease, they will begin to truly interact with each other. This is one sign of healthy discussion.

13. Don't be afraid of controversy. It can be stimulating! If you don't resolve an issue completely, don't be frustrated. Move on and keep it in mind for later. A subsequent study may solve the problem.

14. Periodically summarize what the group has said about the passage. This helps to draw together the various ideas mentioned and gives continuity to the study. But don't preach.

15. Don't skip over the application questions at the end of each study. It's important that we each apply the message of the passage to ourselves in a specific way. Be willing to get things started by describing how you have been affected by the study.

Depending on the makeup of your group and the length of time you've been together, you may or may not want to discuss the "Respond" section. If not, allow the group to read it and reflect on it silently. Encourage members to make specific commitments and to write them in their study guide. Ask them the following week how they did with their commitments.

16. Conclude your time together with conversational prayer. Ask for God's help in following through on the commitments you've made.

17. End on time.

Many more suggestions and helps are found in *The Big Book on Small Groups*, *Small Group Leaders' Handbook* and *Good Things Come in Small Groups* (IVP). Reading through one of these books would be worth your time.

Study Notes

Study 1. Low Self-Esteem. Psalm 139:13-16.

Purpose: To find our self-worth in that fact that we are created uniquely by God, rather than allowing the world to form our self-esteem.

Open. It may be hard for some people in your group to answer this question. Encourage everyone to try. Some of the people who are more willing to answer the question can help by giving suggestions to others in the group about what areas they think they are gifted in. Afterward, take time to reflect on the experience.

Question 2. Looking carefully at this passage, we can see indications that God is part of our past, present and future. In verses 13 and 15 we are told that God was present when we were created. Verse 14 is written in the present as the author praises God. And verse 16 suggests that God has our future in mind as well.

Question 3. "Inmost being" in Hebrew literally means "kidneys." In the Hebrew culture this phrase would have been understood as referring to the center of emotional and moral sensitivity.

Question 4. The first part of the question is designed to help people appreciate the significance of being a "work of God."

Question 6. The second part of this verse could be interpreted in a number of ways. One possibility is that God knows the span of our lives—that is, when we will die. A second possibility would be that God has a specific and detailed plan for each of us. You may come down on either end of this spectrum or at varying points in between.

The reference to God's book is a common motif in the Old Testament. The image is of God "keeping records of events in his realm in the way that earthly kings do, see 56:8; 87:6; 130:3; 139:16; Ne 13:14; Da 7:10; see also Ex 32:32-33" (*The NIV Study Bible*, Kenneth L. Barker, gen. ed. [Grand Rapids, Mich.: 1985], p. 838).

Don't let the second part of the question pull you off on a tangent about God's will. Find encouragement that God does have purposes for us—however specific—and move on to application.

Study 2. Discontent. Psalm 77:1-15.
Purpose: To persevere through a period of discontent to find contentment in God.

Question 3. He remembers God's past graciousness and then is increasingly confused and frustrated by God's seeming failure to respond.

Question 5. The psalmist recalls God's actions on behalf of Israel.

Question 7. God is called "the Most High" (v. 10), holy and great (v. 12). He is described as doing miracles (vv. 11, 14) and "mighty deeds" (v. 12). He displays his power (v. 14), has a "mighty arm" (v. 15) and redeems his people (v. 15).

Question 8. This passage calls us to meditate on who God is and what he has done for us individually and corporately.

Study 3. Gossip. James 3:3-12.
Purpose: To recognize the devastating power of the tongue in order to gain control over it.

Open. Allow plenty of time to focus on these questions. They are important in opening the way to seeing how gossip is a part of our lives.

Question 1. The comparisons are of the bit in a horse's mouth that turns the animal (v. 3), the small rudder that steers a large ship (v. 4), the small tongue that makes great boasts (v. 5), the spark that catches the forest on fire, and the tongue that corrupts the whole body (v. 6).

Question 2. The comparisons in verses 3-6 reveal the dramatic, large-scale damage which is done by small "slips" of the tongue.

Question 3. Our evil talk inflames our evil thoughts. Eventually, we may allow our talk to convince us that we are justified in taking evil actions (beyond gossip) against another. Worst yet, our talk is likely to influence those we gossip with in the same ways.

Question 4. The words that come out of our mouths are a reflection of our sinful hearts and minds. To that extent we will never be "tame." However, if we open ourselves to God, he will take control of our sin through the power of the Holy Spirit.

Question 5. Verses 9 and 10 tell us that out of our mouths come both praises and curses. However, verses 11-12 go on to show that this is an impossible situation. A fig tree cannot bear olives! If these verses feel too overwhelming, you may want to end by reading James 3:13-18, which shows how God empowers us and gives us the wisdom we need to change.

Study 4. Bitterness. Ephesians 4:25-32.

Purpose: To understand what bitterness is and how to handle anger before it becomes bitterness.

Open. It is important to recognize that anger is not necessarily a bad emotion. Often it is a very healthy response to an unhealthy situation. The issue is, then, how we express our anger. Do we own our emotions and try to find the source of our anger? Do we gently and lovingly confront those we are angry with? Or do we let anger fester within us? It is anger which is left undealt with that becomes bitterness—a negative response.

Question 1. The negative behaviors include speaking falsely (v. 25), sinning in anger (v. 26), stealing (v. 27), talking in an unwholesome manner (v. 29), grieving the Spirit (v. 30), being bitter, having rage and anger, brawling and holding malice.

The positive behaviors include speaking truthfully (v. 25), doing something useful and giving to those in need (v. 28), building others up (v. 29), being kind, compassionate and forgiving each other (v. 32).

Question 2. Disagreements within church families range from items of doctrinal importance to worship styles to how the church should be decorated. Sometimes we get our feelings hurt in the midst of such debates but fail to express our anger because we think that good Christians don't get angry. But this isn't true. And when we refuse to deal with our anger, then we are alienated from the person we are angry with. These kind of patterns cannot be a part of a healthy Christian community.

Many people come from dysfunctional families in which anger is never expressed (but out of which comes a great deal of bitterness). Within the church family we have a new opportunity to develop healthy patterns. The church should be a functional family.

Question 3. These verses show us that our anger affects the larger community of faith and may create an opening for evil to gain a hold over the church.

You may stumble over verse 28. It doesn't seem to fit in with the other verses at first glance. However, it fits into the larger context Paul is addressing—Christian community life.

Question 4. Notice that verse 26 suggests that we can be angry. The NRSV translation reads, "Be angry . . ." The key issue in healthy confrontation is to own your feelings—and to consider their appropriateness carefully. Sometimes a strong response may be triggered unknowingly by someone. Consider whether you are upset primarily by the situation at hand or by some past experience—before reacting.

The person who has been hurt should also be careful not to accuse the other, but to describe his or her own feelings clearly. For some this may mean allowing a "cooling" period before confrontation to ensure that you will speak calmly and without offense. Often the worst possible response is to do nothing. The feelings will fester and grow into bitterness.

Question 5. You may wish to skip this question if you feel that it has already been covered.

Question 6. You may want to look back at your definition of the difference between anger and bitterness to answer this question. One critical test is to consider whether expressing anger will improve the current or future relationship(s) involved.

Study 5. Lust. Ephesians 5:1-10.

Purpose: To understand what lust is and when and how it is most likely to affect us individually.

Open. Notice that there are examples of "lust" for a marriage partner here. Within marriage, lust can be a healthy and natural response that is part of our God-given sexuality.

Question 1. The commands are as follows: "Be imitators of God" (v. 1), "live a life of love" (v. 2), "among you there must not be even a hint of sexual immorality . . . impurity, or of greed" (v. 3), no "obscenity, foolish talk or coarse joking" (v. 4), "let no one deceive you" (v. 6), "do not be partners with them" (v. 7), "live as children of light" (v. 8), and "find out what pleases the Lord" (v. 10).

Questions 2-3. These early verses set up a contrast with the sins outlined in the later verses. Lust makes people into objects of our desires. True love values people as individuals with unique worth aside from what they can do for us.

Question 4. Depending on denominational affiliation, ethnicity and upbringing, this may mean very different things to people. Encourage everyone to express their views, and affirm them in that.

Question 6. Be specific about what "foolish talk" and "coarse joking" mean in how we behave (without using offensive details).

Question 7. Notice that verse 5 categorizes lustful thought and conversation as idolatry.

Question 9. Be specific about how you need to reform your thoughts and actions to avoid lust.

Study 6. Passivity. 2 Timothy 1:6-12.

Purpose: To recognize how passivity is a sin that keeps us from serving God, and to empower people to boldly follow Christ.

Question 1. Notice the use of "ashamed" and "power."

Question 3. "Gifts are not given in full bloom; they need to be developed through use" (*NIV Study Bible,* p. 1844).

Question 4. Take time to dwell on each of these words and how their presence in your life empowers you through the Spirit.

Question 7. Sometimes we may be afraid to claim Jesus because we fear suffering. However, these verses give us courage to claim the sufferings of Christ as a privilege, acknowledging that he has suffered for us. We can take Paul as our model in this.

Study 7. Worry. Joshua 1:1-9.

Purpose: To show how worry must be put aside in order for us to follow God.

Open. Worries must not be taken lightly. Encourage the group to listen carefully to each other's concerns, avoiding pat answers and advice-giving. Answers will come later in the study.

Question 1. Moses has recently died. (The book of Joshua picks up where Deuteronomy ends.) Joshua has been chosen as Moses' replacement. These instructions from the Lord echo Moses' instructions to Joshua in Deuteronomy 31:1-8. Joshua is about to lead his people into the Promised Land—a goal they have been waiting for through forty years of living in the desert.

Question 3. There are promises in verses 3, 5, 6, 8 and 9.

Question 7. Return to the concerns named in the opening questions. This is an opportunity to put those concerns before God. Encourage the group to name their concerns during a time of prayer.

Study 8. Materialism. Ecclesiastes 5:10-20.

Purpose: To understand how materialism creeps into our lives so that we can see how we need to redefine our value systems.

Open. Some possible definitions of materialism are "using material things to gain power," "material goods are ends instead of means," "material things become a measuring stick for our self-worth," "we have a continual need for more and more," or "living for worldly things." Some may not know how to respond to the second question. Affirm that they are still learning about Scripture. The study will help them discover what the Bible says about wealth.

Question 1. Loving wealth (v. 10), obtaining more things than we need (v. 11) and hoarding (v. 13) are described in negative terms.

Question 2. When money and possessions are accumulated for their own sake (beyond what is needed to live), they only cause worry and a dissatisfaction which prompts the desire to have even more.

Question 3. Most of us have experienced the problem of "never having enough." For example, we may find that we can live on a certain income, but when a raise in salary comes, we find that that money disappears just as quickly as the rest.

Question 4. In verse 12 the laborer is contrasted with the rich man. The passage suggests that labor is good for body and soul.

Question 5. The evil described in both verses 15 and 16 is that we cannot "take it with us" after death. A real understanding of these verses is that materialism is not a worthy goal in life, because riches do not last or ultimately satisfy.

Question 6. In verses 18-20 God is brought into the picture. When we know that everything we have is a gift from God, we are able to enjoy what we are given. Without God, we will never be satisfied with what we have.

Question 8. Although this passage deals with how we think about money, our philosophy directly affects what we do with our money. Don't let the group fall into the trap of just assuming that God wants them to be wealthy—as long as they give him the credit. Encourage people to consider how they can live in a way that shows that they are not interested in accumulating or hoarding money.

Study 9. People-Pleasing. Galatians 1:6-10.

Purpose: To see how we can fall into the trap of focusing more on pleasing people than on God.

Open. This self-test may bring out some deep issues revolving around self-image and the need for love and affirmation. Make sure that people get the support and encouragement they need. Try to keep track of the time as well. Be ready to come back to these issues during your time of prayer and in following weeks.

Question 1. Note the words "astonished," "so quickly," "deserting" (v. 6), "throwing," "pervert" (v. 7), "eternally," "condemned," (v. 8), and "win" (v. 10).

Question 3. The "people" in verse 7 who are perverting the gospel are "Judaizers," Jewish Christians who believed that Old Testament ceremonial rituals (for example, circumcision) had to be followed. By putting these requirements on the Gentile Christians, they overlooked the gospel's message of grace only through Christ.

The Judaizers also argued that "Paul was not an authentic apostle and that out of a desire to make the message more appealing to Gentiles he had removed from the gospel certain legal requirements" (*NIV Study Bible*, p. 1779).

Question 5. If you haven't already covered it, you may also want to ask, "Why do we try to win the approval of people?"

Study 10. Manipulation. 1 Kings 21:1-19.

Purpose: To see the deadly results of falling into the trap of manipulating people and circumstances—even when it is for a "good" cause.

Open. Some examples of manipulative behavior would be using one person to make another jealous; inviting someone over because you want to get the person to help you with something; getting your friends to agree to go to *your* favorite restaurant.

Encourage everyone to respond to the second question. We use manipulative ploys constantly—but are often not even aware of it. Be ready to give examples of manipulative behavior if group members don't see themselves as being manipulators.

Question 1. It seems that Ahab begins well. He presents his request in a direct manner and offers a fair exchange. He seems to expect that he will get what he wants.

Question 2. See Leviticus 25:23 for the Lord's promise. It is not clear whether God actually intended for families to keep a specific plot of land, but this seems to be Naboth's sincere conviction.

Question 4. Jezebel is a much-maligned biblical woman. While she certainly did wrong, Ahab's immature, whiny behavior must not be overlooked.

Question 6. Jezebel's ultimate end was really ugly. See 1 Kings 22:29-38 for the details.

Question 7. Our culture generally encourages men to be bold and straightforward. Women, on the other hand, are considered pushy and aggressive if they follow the very same patterns. Women must resort to quiet manipulation to gain power. While this is an interesting cultural pattern, it does not excuse manipulation!

Question 8. Women may be particularly vulnerable to doing evil "for the sake of" someone they love. Yet, no matter how high our goals may be, it is important that we see that—even when we are trying to help someone we love—manipulation is never the Christlike approach.

Study 11. Jealousy. Genesis 15:2-6; 16:1-6.

Purpose: To see how jealousy affects all of our relationships, especially our relationship with God.

Open. On the question of why jealousy is a problem more frequently experienced by women, Mary Ellen Ashcroft *(Temptations Women Face,* p. 144) suggests an answer:

> We have had fewer opportunities to figure out what we really want, fewer opportunities to make plans to get what we want. Women have been the watchers and waiters: "Will a man come along who will ask me to marry him?" . . . "Will I get pregnant this month?" "When will the baby come?" . . . we are tempted to envy those who have what we so desperately want.

Question 2. The custom of giving the husband the maidservant to solve the problem of barrenness was within the legal code of that time.

Question 3. It is important to note that Sarai was taking matters into her own hands. Her words, "The LORD has kept me from having children," imply that she thinks God is not keeping his promise. In verse 2 we learn that "Abram agreed."

Question 4. Hagar's position was suddenly elevated from servant to childbearer for her master. She lorded her advantage over Sarai. This response probably rose out of Hagar's envy of her mistress's position.

Question 5. In verse 6 Abram basically refuses to deal with the situation himself and turns over all the authority to Sarai.

Question 7. On the surface this may seem to be a unique example of jealousy because of Sarai's and Abram's sinful actions and lack of trust in God. However, it is just when we are rebelling against God that we are most often vulnerable to temptations like jealousy.

Question 9. As suggested in the first open question, admiring someone can be positive. If we put aside jealousy, we can turn envy into a positive emotion that prompts us to develop Christian character. The first step in this change is confessing your feelings about the other person to God. Steadfast prayer for that person will gradually reform your perspective and help you to love the one you're jealous of.

Study 12. Complacency. Hebrews 5:11—6:3.

Purpose: To see how complacency can be a temptation that limits our capacity to serve God and grow in him.

Question 1. These are not new Christians, but older Christians whose spiritual lives are stagnant.

Question 2. The recipients of the letter are described as spiritually sluggish and lazy. See also 6:12.

Question 3. Notice particularly in 5:13 that they are "not acquainted with the teaching about righteousness." Also, by implication, they cannot "distinguish good from evil" (5:14).

Question 4. Six fundamental doctrines they need to leave behind are mentioned—repentance, faith in God, baptism, laying on of hands (in connection with ordination, healing and blessing), resurrection of the dead, and eternal judgment.

According to Ray Stedman, these beliefs "do not represent anything but the barest beginnings of Christian faith. . . . These transitional truths lead from Jewish beliefs and practices to a full sharing in Christ." They must move from "head knowledge to heart knowledge" (*Hebrews,* IVP New Testament Commentary Series [Downers Grove, Ill.: Inter-Varsity Press, 1992], p. 71). In other words, they must put their knowledge into practice.